DONATION PLATE

Chase Cohl

Donation Plate

Chase Cohl

ISBN: 978-1-66787-605-4

CONTENTS

I. HEART

II. BODY

HEART

On Sunday Morning

I woke to find
I'd written a series of names

a list
those I've loved
those I wish to love
yours was at the top

I don't remember writing
as if from a dream
pre-sleep
post-drunk

considered smoking a cigarette
but instead, I thought of you
& felt a calmness

if you see me
be sure to say hello .

the ghost .

Your face is haunting
my dreams at night.

Sometimes I find you
in the water
soft, kind.
Sometimes you are a storm
cold, dark.

Your voice
remains the same,
your eyes always dance
          for me (alone).

You tell me I'm special
call me baby, Baby
like
you never did before.
Like I found myself
wish you would.

I don't tell you anything,
because you already know.

Game of Dice.

Gave you my body
when I wanted to give my heart.

Ah, god damn it.

Monday

Against my better judgement
I let him come over.
Talk about making him a tea
but I don't even care enough
to turn on the kettle.

He tries to touch me
on the couch he
wraps me in this old, moth-hole
covered blanket

My mind goes to you
how you'd call it a dream.

Do you miss my touch
my breath on your skin
that worn country skin
older than its years
like you were ?

I still feel this temptation
urgent, pulsing
to give you
all of myself.

What he wants too badly
he will never have.

England

you were gone
before I opened my eyes
I knew the way you know
a wave will crash
before it does

we made love but
we were fire & water

(you saw it first)

sometimes it feels worse
to be right

the funny thing about the sea
& men like you
how they always return

listen closely

My heart is not
a summer read

it is
a bible.

revisionist history.

Over the months we spent
there were countless times
deep in frenzy
immersed in covers
my heart wanted to cry
I love you
but somehow the only words
my mouth could muster
were *don't stop.*

lovers & crushes.

I hope this finds you well.
I had a notion this morning
over a cup of dandelion tea
before I walked my tired feet
down the mountainside
in an attempt to heal my brain
perhaps from the injury
you have made
that maybe, for some reason or another
you might like to know
your girlfriend
stalks me
on the internet.

a small thank you

As it turns out

the best lovers I ever had

were also the best

listeners.

—

the secret to pleasing women in bed.

honey.

I've spent an awful lot of time
of late convincing myself
I am unworthy of love
because I hurt someone's heart

Afterward
while he ran around
spreading his wounded seed
making love to any who would claim him
the way men tend to

I became a monk
I took on all the worries of the world
I repeat my mantra
Unworthy, unworthy, unworthy
the way women tend to

As he lay his head
between their perfect thighs
alabaster & honeyed
he would tell them how he hurt
until my name became the poison
on his saccharine lips

He told me I always acted
like he wasn't good enough
I said back
later, aloud to myself
(the way I do these days)
Honey,
that's where I live

Bees come to die at my bedside
daily, when the windows are left open
for him, I think *enough* was the word
for me it was *act*

I cover myself in honey now
morning noon & night
to bring the sweetness back
& am learning that

sometimes all we really need
is just an
excuse for our pain.

Distaste.

Hate me all you want
throw rocks at my doorstep
tell everyone who will listen
that you don't care
shout it into the skies

I'll be over here
quiet and
loving you from afar
cv8765432

salt water.

Today we got caught
in a lightning storm
while searching for
crocodiles & other such
prehistoric creatures
in this abandoned zoo
dense & lush
like we wished we were

Thought about salt
water while getting drenched
by the deluge
hoping for a cleanse to
bring some redemption
I let it soak me

& wondered what you
might have said
how you'd approach this moment
with adventure
with love
roll your glorious head
back in laughter
squint your sapphire eyes

I tried to learn from you
had a daydream of clasped
palms in the overgrowth
though you're not here
too little too late
I suppose.

Breakneck

If it is alright with the cosmos
I continue writing letters
just to set them on fire
the way I did myself
burn them into nothingness & hope the ashes
somehow make it to the end of the cigarette
I picture you pulling when you appear in my dreams
most nights

I have become so brutally, deeply, softly woman
it is impossible to surmise
whether absolution
could help me now

You must see these days
I am byzantine pottery fresh from the kiln
come in close
you can watch the cracks
who line the insides
let the love leak out

There was a young man
who treated my body
as though it were
a throw away
copper penny from the street
picked up, discarded
my heart fell prey
to feeling something more breakneck

He is gone
forgot me like the nothing everyone said
the way I feel you try

I should've been prudent to see
who would share my torturous secrets
without so much as asking
how this heart might feel
I am older now
I am wiser now

From bed

I thought I smelled
black coffee brewing
half-blind & bone-tired
floated into the kitchen
with hope it may have all been
an atrocious dream
that you'd be standing
six months ago where
I left the best version of us
it was empty

I received word
from a man who has imagined
but never known
the curve of my body
the devious tooth continually trying to flee coop
telling me I was deep
these days, if to indulge just so
I am an infinite reservoir.

I pitched back
and thought of you
held a man's hand
and thought of you
exchanged sweltry glims
and thought of you
kissed someone's mouth
and thought of you
I saw your family
and thought, oh fuck

Last night, Sister told me
while wandering down Elizabeth street
recalling nervous frenzy and all of the men
palms clenched like handcuffs
I'd loved on that block
that you were no good for me
too credulous too thespian
plus I never liked the taste of your tongue so much
I concur

Yet still, so often
I think of that August morning
you woke before dawn
just to rustle me out of bed
so ardent so quiet
the way my mother used to
and realize you felt like family once .

Education.

The last time
I slept in this bed
you were here
in all your beauty
under the crooked beams
the lowly slice of crown molding
which frustrated you so
and why I don't have enough books
although you don't read anyway

Tell me, lover
how can one person
of so little years
an atomic life
know enough
not to educate themselves
live enough
not to explore in language
and *feel enough*
not to fall in love with fancy
the way I was so intensely born to do

I saged the place today
envisioned myself burn it to the ground
her name, that of the earth
a sister of the woods, sister of mine
with softly kind eyes & the kind of hair
other girls cry for not having
she loved you
brought life into this house
with the gift of motherhood

all you brought was melancholy
& an attempt to share this live
you could not possibly want
you could not possibly survive
with a heart like yours

The last time we spoke
you said you'd do anything for me
swore it unto the stars in heaven
I never asked a thing
for wanting is trickery
but wonder now
if I may request one small kindness
stop telling everyone
that I do not care
that you hate me with the simple truth is
I could not possibly survive your life.

Do not take my name in vain.

An open letter.

My body betrayed my heart

when I saw your face

on the internet

& felt the mere sight of you

steeped in all your motherfucker glory

still get me excited

below the belt.

–

chivalry lives one thousand miles away
from your blue eyes.

I didn't know you long enough

Of course

you thought this was all about you

grow up, silly man

I let you touch my skin

not my heart.

The body betrays

Then
after months of daydreams
and writing this book for you
I finally saw your face
wanted to tell you so many things
of the hurt and the love
the deep hole of madness
I've gone into
come back from
in your honour
wanted so much to
ask of your heart
your worship of the world
to shout my love for you
from the rooftop
in an exorcising frenzy
when I realize
you do not want to hear these declarations
so they become swallowed
and one more terrible time

my imprisoned tongue
whispers in agony
"Good to see you"

–

what a goddamn coward

cooking for one

I have to admit
It isn't really much fun
without you
here.

No offense.

I took myself
on a date today
to the sea
to remind myself
of you & the ebb
& the flow

Because we
are strangers now

There were no flowers
but I dug my tired toes
in that luscious warm sand
without any words
to spoil the view

A moment of perfection
and Boy!
was it romantic
when all at once
the truth crashed into me
like a wondrous deluge
that maybe, just maybe
I am the best boyfriend
I've ever had.

BODY

something like liquid.

and tonight
all at once
I realized that all
of the romantic love
I have ever felt
in the fleeting decades
of my adult life
has led me to water and
still left me parched

—

Good love should hydrate your heart.

Quenching thirst.

Baby
you say I don't care
think I won't mind
from the bottom of this
shallow well the truth is
I can share tales to
everyone but you
of the honey which flows
from the endless crevices of
this small figure
this body
that somehow you claimed
in the time since you
left me heaving
on the bed
windows open
unable to breathe
in your absence
I wrote you a letter
I wrote you five hundred
I wrote you a goddamn book
you want me to see
so here I am
cackling bloody madness
from the mountain top
like a feral coyote
until I lose my voice.

I see you
Okay?

Temporary blindness.

Sometimes I find
myself wishing to the
perfect nighttime sky
that I had cataracts
in my eyes
like that numinous owl
otherworldly magic type
for the sole purpose
of not having to see
your goddamn face
and feel so much
of this ever so
exhausting thing called
feeling.

the true.

whoever

loves

you

will

be

better

for

it .

I thought of you this morning

I woke near the sea
and thought of you
not because there was
some baronial sunrise
but because
of the stillness.

My bones have
become just exhausted enough
to act frantically
yet the tides lullaby
enduring in the early light
sang to me
sedated me
the way only
your presence could.

A million miles away
by some other nameless
body of water
you are falling asleep
thinking of me too.

modern sex.

touch but don't look .

company.

I couldn't help
but feel my heart drop
when you let your heart
that tender thing I
shattered like a china
teacup it had cracks
before don't get me wrong
but they were filled
with fine French bergamot
stains who have since
vanished I give those spots
to someone else now I
play the long game and anyway
when you let your heart
that tender thing
in the company of
women I know who cannot
possibly heal or scrub
those dainty streaks
the ones who never
get their hands dirty for
fear of ruining their
feminine fingertips the best
parts of you the ones
who should be cultivated
and farmed like
solid pieces of land are
made from the salt
of the earth and while
I understand why you would
go that way I can't help
but wish you wouldn't.

an anonymous letter after the weekend

i felt you
before i saw you

you always seem to move in
like the start of a new
season a little bit
then all at once
the way they say people fall
in love sometimes in
folklore in this case
shown as the quivering of
these clenched and swollen summer
fingers plus my mouth froze
up i stared
in those goddamn eyes
and since my tongue
usually sprite and soaked
in morning dew wit in
the smoothest honey
you ever tasted twists

when you feel near
these days mostly i
just write and you'd never
in any way recognize this need
in me to distinctly
not capitalize my i's
when writing of you

though those delicate hands are
surely clasped inside hers
by now and likely will never
be able to untangle myself
enough in your presence
again all this to say
i thought you should know
in the only way my mouth will let me
i think you are just
that
glorious.

One two.

He used to push me
against the wall
in moments of fervor, passion
now the man won't make
my eyes I wait & wait
let me get this straight
men are scared
of women now?

Waterside.

chapter one.

while eating a summer
plum I saw a photograph
of you with your
new love studied
the face that was once
the only thing I ever wanted
to see for some sort
of familiarity she looked
happy you looked
different you have a moustache
now like some old cowboy
in a western film and your
northern heart always
liked the earthy/granola type
anyhow.

chapter two.

Mother and I agree
you'll probably marry
this one I can't explain
why my bones told me so
but when two people go
to war like we did baby
no matter how long
we do not speak there
will always live a little bit of
you inside me.

chapter three.

I search long and hard for
some semblance of the person
I loved abyssal and wild
so many times
it nearly killed me
without any luck or
belonging I realize
though I'll always miss our sex
and the excited longing in
your tired blue eyes
no matter how much time
passes through the years
when it comes to you
I never find what I'm looking for.

to be fair

after months of
being touched poorly
by a man who did not
know the softness
this body needs
his hands listened.

France, etcetera

After all the time
spent together rolled
like fresh breakfast pastry
layered in one another
it takes a mere photograph
to realize quickly
I'd forgotten your face

I search your sun worn
skin and kissed eyelashes
for recognition
it does not come
and yet I feel you
beside me in a way
words cannot express
your breath is light
and with me always
like a wafting scent
fresh from the oven
each morning when I wake

is this what they call
soul?

short love//
a brief romance

One hour
can last a lifetime.
One day,
eternity.

possession.

I see you
with that furrow
the face you make
like spoiled beer

in a second you
come to realize
that I have
let
you
go

after you
treated me
like only an option

–

now you call me baby

the easiest egg to crack

He tells
with such sincere
conviction it could
break your heart
how he tried hard
gave all his might
to date me.

I recall it well
the flirt dripping
in sarcasm all interaction
inebriated I remember
a walk through
the rain to one single
laughter soaked
night in a hotel bed.

The secret here about
the modern man is
he never actually
asked me
on
a
date.

funny

I think of you
and just like that
I'm home again.

A letter from the reader

I watch you shut
your heart down
as if you were
closing a book

Don't you know
by now you must
leave it open
to be read?

–

your heart will tell you what kind of love it needs

I see myself in you

I watch you squirm
whenever the real
warmth directs your way

who broke you
who taught you that
the easiest way
to live your life
was devoid of hysteric bliss

don't you understand
the heart was made to love?

in the spirit of honesty,

because we do not speak

It was really just
a peculiar little thing
like reliving the faintest
of childhood memories
when overnight
autumn swept in

maybe it was the passing
of that final summer sky
or the brisk kiss
in the North Ontario
air, the way I described
time & again but
somehow by morning

I couldn't stop thinking
of you.

I know why they call it fall

When autumn comes
I picture you
in an apple orchard

young, squinting to keep
the glistening sun from
the smile lines by your eyes

you remind me of
my favourite love
the one who broke me
and yet by nature
I cannot hate

I hope I am not
that one to you
who hurt you so that
you cannot see
the immaculate good
that grew between us
among the macouns

I woke you early
and remember well
spilling jars of tea
on my clothes in the woods
when nobody knew where
we were, you
free and so full on life
rolling your glorious
head back in laughter .

And in the end

when the fight had
subsided no more
sounds to be made
all we had left
in the lingering breath
of soon autumn come
was the love

A literary hangover.

To all the men
I sent along
a tender word of prayer
or maybe even just the
most sincere of compliments
within the hours of dawn.

I must bestow the truth
the wine it spoke
not me
so keep my words
a gift to you
to leave your ego bright
yet hear they had
no depth.

The woman gets lonely sometimes.

my love is a garden

this love in me
that eats at the bone
of my innermost self
blinding in its radiance,
ardent in its passion
OH, you should see the colours
would thrive best amongst
the flowers
like maybe some sort
of wild medieval plant
a fig leaf, a thorny rose
bush perhaps

It too, needs space
to grow, to blossom
needs deep rooted care
water and seasonal change

The botanists instructions
remain fairly clear
if neglected or smothered so
the leaves will turn
before your eyes
and wilt in only
this tragic, decomposing
way the most natural
tings in the world
are known to do

No
if you neglect
this precious plant
do not come searching
for it will bloom
a most beautiful flower
the kind to bring you
to your knees
but also the kind
that has learned to live
without you

forget – me - not

an open letter, to those who seem to be confused:

Let me be clear
I love you
is not
a pick-up
line.

Donation Plate

I think
I will drive down
to the beach
scream your name
like some church donation
to a plate of froth
a prayer of salvation
into the sea
like I have so many
motherfucking holy days
this past year
until it takes my voice
tell it over until the rolling waves
become you
and jump right in

BRAIN

630

the sky this morning
when I woke
it looked like blood

red, deep wanton red

as if
every faulty word
all of the heart hurt
scattered across these mountains
finally caught up
and Mother Nature cried
tears, burning, fervent
blood red .

It was beautiful .
It was the most beautiful
little thing
like nothing from a photograph .

And then again,
like the quiet hum of
a night light,
instantaneously, I wish
you were here .

wildfire.

California is burning
and all I can think
of is
you.

the superiority complex.

On a foggy mountain morning
waiting for too much coffee

I notice a father & his daughter
carrying a young child
like a prized possession
at the country fair

A handsome couple
freshly fucked, braiding fingers
she wipes something off
of his chin
glances around as if to
claim the moment
an intimacy hoarder

The lonely old poet
spouting dime store proverb
ten cent rhymes
about sex, about god

The others waiting
for their turn
to be heard & I think maybe

Life is just people
going in public
to show off
the things that they have made
in private.

Some Sunday in March .

And so,
look what you did

Love,
with that salted skin
you rust like an anchor
trapped under the sea
for a time

You tried to hold me too tight
like grains of sand
didn't you learn
silly child
you cannot grip sand in your palm
without it slipping through
your fingers too

These days
I have conversations with you
your memory
while driving
aloud in the car

This morning
we talked about airport pickups
how I hate them, the pressure
that when I picked you up
by the autumn sunrise
after losing my way
in the terminal roundabout
I had forgotten your face
unknowingly and was caught

breathless
from your beauty
that when you picked me up
I couldn't kiss you
too fucked up too scared
too deep in self loathing
to let someone like you be tender
with someone like me

The house feels empty without you in it
my flowers wilt in boredom
that I found myself back here
alone
again

I know you'd be happy to hear
I can finally write about you
after all these months

I wrote a piece about you
I thought it would make you laugh
but without you here
it just feels cruel

I only wanted to make you laugh

Musings on being back in Canada.

I suppose that I must be
some certain kind of flower
for I, too
burgeon in the soil
where I was grown,.

7 a.m. , these days.

I think of you still as much as ever
of your cracked & sun-soaked skin
sleepy eyes
how I ran my fingers over them
while you slept.

Yesterday
I made a breakthrough
while spreading jam on toast
wanted so much to tell you
that I whispered it into my pillow at midnight
hoping somehow that
it would make it through to yours.

I think I feel differently now
you do too.
I am beginning to dream again, yet
if I close my eyes, I can still hear your laugh
picture you pulling on a cigarette
picture you close to me
though I'm not sure I want to.

Darling, we were good at making plans
took hopeful promise made a childish mess.

You should know,
the women you slight
still check in on me day in, day out
like vultures in the sun.

I think about going to the desert
succumbing myself to them
their rancorous hunger
has become a quiet hum
in the back of my mind.

I miss you but
you feel like a stranger now,
& somewhere in my depth
buried in the honey that flows inside of me
out of me
I am beginning to forgive myself.

I think of you still as much as ever
maybe even more.

Eckhart Tolle

told me that
all pain stems from the ego
the deep I, he calls it

Said wherever you are
is where the entire universe
has conspired to bring you
into this exact moment

The one thing
I can't seem to grasp
with all of my brains
this expensive Swiss
boarding school education

Why do I have to learn
my lessons this hard
over, over again
why must I be hit on the head
with a cast iron fry pan
like the ones you
so proudly hold
and why my mistakes
were too much for you
to be here with me

I never said I was perfect
I told you I was a mess
I never said I was in love
with you, a little bit

These words
those heedless, silly sounds
sat on my tongue
rotting my taste buds
while I watched you
writhe inside of me
trying to access pieces of my spirit
in discomfort
because I couldn't let you
have that so soon

And then you were gone
left to boil
in a bathtub of your own loathing
while Eckhart and I
drink our troubles away
talk about the universe
the stars in the sky
and miss you so much.

Barrier.

We do not speak
the words so
I write to you in whispers
in seedlings moved
by the wind
after all
you still understand love
don't you?

Springtime and

These god-for-saken cherry blossoms
have awoken something inside of me

I'm coming out of this self-inflicted chrysalis
hour by hour
& you don't haunt me the way
you once did

Not so much, at least
this brain, nearly drowned by memories
but my appetite
for weathered country skin
weakness for a lazy drawl, cunning mind
never satiates.

I am so profoundly woman now
it brings me to tears
I think I'll have my cake & eat it too,.

If

Back in California
when I make the pilgrimage
west to the flowered house
at an eventual time
(not now)
Returned to find
upon arrival
you living in my home
after no words spoken
for these torturous eons

I think all I could do
take this Herculean gulp
of glorious breath
and say
What took you so long ?

Reflections.

Earlier this evening
I caught myself in the mirror
cleansed from a river water shower

Grappled with the concept
of my pale and naked body
being one day seen by somebody else
worshipped by someone else
aside from you, since you
struggling with the words you
tried so much, to convince me of

Traced the curve of my hip
the constellation of freckles
I pioneered so fiercely to adore
in the years of my youth
(when I was about your age)
the worn silk skin, which carries
all this memory

Stepped back to notice
my only possession
in the mirror
that mirror you hung so graciously
while I yelled some nonsense about being late
look what you did
you made it so that
every time I look at myself
I think of you

As I stared at myself
I said aloud
I love you
I love you
to the end of the light

Earlier this morning
I shattered the mirror
seven years of bad luck
got nothing on me

–

It has taken me months to realize
I am just as beautiful
without you here

Build me an orchard

Did you ever consider
how many hours it might take you
to grow an apple
from start to finish?
from seed to crunch
the astonishing levels of labour & love
how much patience, how many rainstorms
how many pegs planted in the soil

Today I wore the overalls
the ones you loved so much
same you consoled me in
while I cried for the loss
of fallen kin
near the most darling of orchards
on a warm October afternoon
back when I could not let you console me
could not let you touch me
bruised from all the failure
& being dropped so many times
or picked too soon

A man I met told me
I was born in these
weathered skins, and miles away
I catch sight of you
rolling your head back in laughter
with mine as the most distant, dismal memory.

I thought you should know
for whatever it's worth
he's nice to me, now
the way they always are
in the beginning
the way you were
back when you thought
I was simply unripe, sweetly damaged
ambrosial & darling albeit a harmless worm hole
indistinguishable to the untrained eye

Did I fall in love with you in those apple orchards
did I fall in love with the apple orchards because you were there
is love a contagion effect
in either case if time permits
I would like to grow us just one

Beverly.

As I sit
on Beverly boulevard
fucking Beverly
the word I've come to shutter
at watching traffic
go by there is a girl
with a tiny dog
sobbing into her friend's
pale and bony shoulders
about healing crystals
for pets and animal
reiki while casually pondering
which coffee to get

I miss New York.

Freedom of speech.

it has come to my attention
that while you are beautiful
and damn you make
me laugh
when by my side
my dear
I really do love you
from the bottom of my
heart well
but its time I let you know
I hate you
on the internet.

I knew him once

the kind
of man
who can teach
you things
remaining still
soft yet humble
taste a rose
taste you
carry your weight
a boy who
loves everybody
but hates everything.

modern love.

while I sip
this five-dollar cup
of mediocre coffee
whose taste my tongue
has begun to repel
I watch this couple
seemingly sort of
sweet and intertwined
engulfed in screens
she rests her lovely
blonde mane
against his warm rounded
shoulder without
making a wince
of eye contact and
when he makes some
sort of joke she
laughs hard
but never looks him
in the eye for
a solitary moment and
I begin to wonder
if maybe romance now
is just having someone
to text near.

what ever happened to romance?

mostly I spend all of my time
these days alone and
some moments ponder if
life will always be this way
cause maybe though
I could manifest the man
who would always hold me near
love me till I die
for only $7.99 per month
and a dope Instagram.

The truth of the matter.

The thing was
without the glances
accidental finger brush
telling anyone who cared
the other's face was
absolute pure
and bloody magic
a favourite thing
these hypothetical
day dream conversations
of when things could
work out in love
the way I hoped
so much they would
but never spoke the word
the thoughts
inside these two small minds
who, trapped in bubbles
birth the world
without those things
we were really

just friends

BREAST

feminine mystique.

I shoot awake at 4:30am
to chase down
cold spots in the mattress
& wonder why
I'm not thinner

Better
more like her, like them
why when my body folds
into itself it
lumps like a sack of
small potatoes
these days when I try to
bend to anyone

I feel myself shrug
maybe I was not made to bend

There is more
important work to be done here
my mother's practicality interrupts
plus in the North
this sack//body would be hidden
under heavy wools
much of my life
that is what I was built
for anyway

My hands are strong
they were made to work
my wit is sharp
to muse to surmise
body
not that of my mother, nor my grandmother
mine alone
grown to make love
freckled and flawed and glorious and
changing by the hour

Not like these lithe Texan women
skinny southern belles
an image of wheat comes to mind
blowing in a field
lovely, pliable
grown to be turned into someone else

still why this need to compare
could you love this body too
like you love hers
do I even care
do I care so much
probably not, I answer
to all four
(though I know that is untrue)
I remember the card reading
said be careful
what you wish for

Yet here I lay
listless in this strange land
where I've never quite fit
wondering at 5:39am
what would make me worthy of your desire
your heart
if maybe I should stop eating carbs
for good this time
if I'll ever feel
at home again
in the arms of any man
if I should grow two long braids
wait around from them to turn
a blazing silver
& how in the fuck
this country I *chose*
has a jester for a president
young people don't care about books
nobody here seems to comprehend
how to actually love another
& somewhere far away
the last male white rhino has died

Then whether you
could forget all of that
for a moment
want me show it prove me right
above all
if I could want myself over
again & again
A woman's work is never done.

the body complex.

The great truth of my life
ever since I was small
I have known
without a doubt
that I was grown to be a mother
given life
to give life

& yet at thirty
there is still so much to learn

In stead
I hold imaginary communion
with all of the children
yet to be born
to this body they'll call home

I've been thinking about womanhood
a lot lately

how we expel so much
loathing the thing that gives life
the most miraculous little thing

maybe our own beauty
simply frightens us too much
& why do we learn to shun
the only thing we've really got

My Canadian-ness, my womanhood & I

have been unnecessarily apologizing
for so many decades now
I think I will banish
the word *sorry* from my vocabulary

I have been on this diet
starvation of the heart and body
I will no longer ask
your pardon, *Sir*
for being so very much alive

Join in on the madness
or leave me be.

No longer do I (a mantra)

I don't need you
to think I'm beautiful
to see my beauty
I don't need you
to think I'm sexy
in order to feel sexy
I don't need you to touch me
to sense shivers of fervency
I don't need you
to tell me I'm special
to notice the alchemy in this body
I don't need you
to tell me I'm smart
to know the depth of my knowledge
I don't need you
to give me your time
to know my worth

I have sacrificed too long at the helm of men like you

Candlelight & Wine

The sweetest girl I know
had a problem of the heart
she spoke of last night
torturous palpitations
over wine, with tea
by candlelight
as her skin glowed
one cup of coffee
and she couldn't breathe
with grace, she recounted
how in order to fix
the broken piece
some medical folk
had to burn a part
of the heart off
in order for her to
sleep through the night
let the blood pump free
so she could take
just one glorious easy breath

How beautiful, I thought
as I fell asleep
if every so often
the best thing
we can do for these
battered, beaten hearts
we keep inside
after years of abuse
from the troubles of life
is set them on fire
and start over again.

Recently:

I broke the mold
shattered these glass shackles
same ones that make women and
this female form of mine
think that in addition to
being born to give life
created to make love
it also cannot survive without
playing strong and tough
laying the most intricate
and gilded brickwork
around her most sensitive parts
keeping it all together
a nod to say hello
doesn't own this earth mother
power that pulses within
like the beat of a war drum
ba-bump ba-bump
the time has come
to let this go

—

I am done trying to be perfect for you
Instead I will just be myself

New Years.

To you
the darling males
whom I have offended
with this
my savage womanhood
I'm sorry
I have no apology

–

no man would lose one wink
doing the things I have done

mothers & children

how can this be
anything but
blinding fidelity
the love for her
after all
she made you
from her body
you were once
a limb she
chose to
set you free.

Glass houses.

an open letter to women
on the internet everywhere :

who broke you
who starved you
who made you feel so
deeply in need of this
attention this
validation that you
are smart that
you are cultured
sexual beautiful
and does this one
tiny little photograph
that can't possibly
express your
fullness your
depth your
brilliance and
the way
you love like a
flush winter's fever
help you sleep
at night

LET THE HEALING BEGIN.

portrait of a female artist.

They only want you
when they can't have you
they only need you
till they get you

It's a subtle dance
the sleight of hand
a power shift so quiet
it can be stolen
in a single syllable

I, myself
too old fashioned
of tender heart
to master this game
the one they play
so unknowingly
it is like watching
a comic tragedy
from the outside in.

and still, we are no closer to love.